Raw Food *detox*

Raw Food *de*tox

Revitalize and rejuvenate with these delicious low-calorie recipes
to help you lose weight and improve your energy levels

Anya Ladra
of Raw Fairies

photography by
William Lingwood

LONDON · NEW YORK

Senior Designer Iona Hoyle
Commissioning Editor Céline Hughes
Head of Production Patricia Harrington
Art Director Leslie Harrington
Editorial Director Julia Charles
Indexer Hilary Bird

First published in 2013 by
Ryland Peters & Small
20–21 Jockey's Fields
London WC1R 4BW
and
519 Broadway, 5th Floor
New York, NY 10012
www.rylandpeters.com

10 9 8 7 6 5 4 3 2 1

Text © Anya Ladra 2013
Design and photographs
© Ryland Peters & Small 2013
Printed in China

ISBN: 978-1-84975-265-7

A CIP record for this book is available from
the British Library.

A CIP record for this book is available from
the US Library of Congress.

Notes
• All spoon measurements are level unless
otherwise specified.

Neither the author nor the publisher can be
held responsible for any claim arising out of
the information in this book. Always consult
your health advisor or doctor if you have
any concerns about your health or nutrition.

The publisher would like to thank
Juiceland Ltd for the kind loan of the
dehydrator used to prepare food for the
photography in this book.
www.juiceland.co.uk

contents

introduction

in the raw

I spent most of my childhood on my grandparents' farm surrounded by fresh, organic food. My fondest memories are of making our own butter and cheese – all unpasteurized – and baking bread. These early experiences became a strong foundation for my interest in health and vitality. Later, I graduated in law and worked for a financial company, but after a while I made the decision to leave the job and move to London to transform my life. Shortly after arriving, I started planning a business that would promote health and allow me to devote my time to my true passions: food and working with colours, flavours, textures and shapes.

In 2007, I founded Raw Fairies, the UK's first raw-food delivery service. We provide home- and office-delivered diet and cleansing detox programmes that are unique, delicious and effective. Clients can order daily drinks and meals that are all free from meat, fish, dairy, wheat, gluten and processed sugar, and generally low GI. By using fresh, organic, plant-based ingredients we provide a diet that is high in nutrients but also low in calories.

People come to us for many different reasons. Generally, they want us to help them cleanse their bodies and lose weight quickly, or they would like to improve and maintain their daily wellbeing. Most of our clients enjoy feeling more energetic, revitalized, brighter and lighter.

By using this book, you should be inspired to introduce raw food into your life and see that it can be done easily, with delicious and surprisingly satisfying results. Hopefully, you will soon find that you can create a complete meal without once using a stove or oven! Imagine sitting down to the meal pictured opposite – Green 'Pad Thai' (page 87), Green Veggie Juice (page 27) and Pecan Cookies (page 136) – and feeling better than ever because your body and mind are being treated to the best that natural food has to offer.

raw benefits

The raw-food diet is based on the belief that the most healthful food for the body is uncooked and not heated above around 48°C/118°F, in order to preserve the enzymes. Enzymes are the life force of food: they are responsible for every metabolic action in the body; they are the catalysts that enable cells to work and chemical reactions to happen without themselves being consumed in the process. Every food contains the perfect mix of enzymes necessary for the body to digest it completely, but cooking above 48°C/118°F destroys these enzymes, forcing our bodies to generate their own. Our body cannot produce the same quality of enzymes as are found naturally, therefore we can't always digest the food properly. Cooking above 48°C/118°F can also kill certain vitamins, such as Vitamin C and folic acid.

A raw-food diet is composed of the purest wholesome ingredients which are unprocessed, unrefined, without synthetic flavourings and preservatives, and because of that, they break down slowly and feed your body with sustained energy.

Raw food can be prepared by chopping, blending, slicing, shredding, dehydrating or juicing, and some of these processes might require advanced planning, for example, nuts and grains might need to be soaked, some seeds are best eaten sprouted, and some dishes need to be dehydrated for several hours.

There are many reasons to include more fresh, raw foods in your diet, no matter what your current starting point. These are just some of the reasons.

* They contain anti-ageing enzymes

* They aid effortless weight loss

* They have better flavour and texture than their cooked counterparts

* They generate super levels of health

* They diminish tiredness

* They provide more nutrients

* They give more energy and endurance

* They promote healthy skin, hair and nails

* They engender better sleep patterns

* They increase mental clarity

* Their high water content prevents dehydration

Getting started

* Start your day with a cup of warm water infused with a slice of lemon, to balance your body's pH (its level of acidity and alkalinity)

* Eat organic produce whenever possible

* Have some raw food with every meal and snack, for example, a salad for lunch and dinner, and a smoothie for breakfast; a balanced diet includes a full spectrum of colours and all five tastes: sweet, salty, sour, pungent/umami and bitter, so go for a variety

* Avoid processed, fast and fried foods

* Reduce the amount of dairy products you eat

* Introduce freshly made vegetable and fruit juices and smoothies to your diet

* Drink plenty of water

* Eat sprouts and algae

* Introduce more dark, leafy greens to your diet, for example, for breakfast have a green smoothie made with ripe, organic fruit and greens – green is the colour of healing

* Start experimenting with new ingredients and recipes

* Change your eating habits slowly to allow your body and lifestyle to adapt; changes made too quickly can put added stress on the body

Even a small increase in the proportion of raw foods in your daily diet can have significant health benefits.

powerhouse ingredients

Fresh ingredients

Buy only organic products when possible. Always wash the fruit and vegetables before starting to prepare them for a dish.

Alfalfa sprouts
Alfalfa is a good source of chlorophyll and vitamins, especially beta-carotene and Vitamin E. Alfalfa sprouts contain digestive-aiding enzymes, amino acids, carbohydrates and minerals.

Avocado
This is one of the most complete foods, with plenty of fibre and the perfect balance of essential fatty acids. See also page 66.

Beet(root)
High in beta-carotene and folic acid, beet(root) helps to cleanse the liver and prevent heart disease when eaten regularly. See also page 105.

Cucumber
This is an excellent diuretic and system cleanser rich in vitamin B, calcium and folic acid. Due to its significant water content, it aids the function of the kidney, liver and pancreas.

Dark green, leafy vegetables
Dark leafy greens, such as kale, rocket/arugula, spinach and watercress are among the most under-consumed but most nutritious vegetables with lots of fibre, enzymes and antioxidants. They are a rich source of iron, potassium, calcium, magnesium, Vitamin C, E and K, and B vitamins. They contain phytonutrients including beta-carotene, lutein and zeaxanthin which protect our cells from damage. They may help protect from heart disease and diabetes. Eat them with a little fat as it helps to promote the absorption of fat-soluble Vitamin K.

Dates
These are rich in dietary fibre, antioxidants such as beta-carotene, lutein, zeaxanthin and tannins, minerals including potassium, calcium, manganese, iron and copper. When eaten, they replenish energy and revitalize the body instantly, due to a high content of simple sugars like fructose and dextrose.

Ginger
Fresh ginger root contains many health-giving essential oils which improve the digestion and have anti-inflammatory and antibacterial properties. It is very rich source of many essential nutrients and vitamins such as Vitamin B6 and B5, and minerals including potassium, copper and manganese.

Kale
The dark green, leafy powerhouse is high in calcium, Vitamin A and C, is a powerful detoxifier and is known as the king of juicing.

Parsley
Parsley is rich in Vitamin A and C, iron, calcium and potassium, as well as chlorophyll. It is valued for its diuretic properties. Add a bunch of fresh parsley whenever you make a fresh vegetable juice.

Spinach
Spinach is rich in Vitamin A and K, folic acid and iron. It also contains flavonoids, compounds that do double duty as antioxidants and cancer-fighters.

Sprouts
Sprouts are some of the most nutritious foods on the planet. They are said to be rich in vitamins, minerals, amino acids and a treasure trove of plant enzymes, which are at their most abundant in the early sprouting stage. When you sprout beans or seeds, what you produce is an enhanced package of the nutrients already present in the original seed. Seeds, beans, nuts and grains such as chickpeas, mung beans, lentils, azuki beans are all easy to sprout at home over a 3–4-day period (see page 16). Only use whole seeds and beans, as split ones will not sprout. See also page 62.

Watercress
Watercress is a rich source of Vitamin A and C, iron and calcium. It plays an important role in combating cancer and some research has shown it to have natural antibiotic properties. Add it to your salads, juices and smoothies on a daily basis. See also page 44.

Storecupboard ingredients

If you are planning to follow a raw-food diet in earnest, it might be useful to stock up on a few key storecupboard ingredients that are often used in the dishes in this book.

Agave nectar

Extracted from the Mexican agave cactus plant, this is about 1.5 times sweeter than table sugar, which means you need to use less to reach the same level of sweetness in a recipe which in turn results in fewer calories. It also has a slightly lower glycemic index than table sugar.

Barley grass powder

This powder is made from the dried young leaves of the barley plant. As with most types of vegetable powders, it is very easily digested by the body. Barley grass contains very large amounts of vitamins such as Vitamin B1, B2, B6, B12, Vitamin C, folic acid, minerals, amino acids, enzymes and living chlorophyll.

Chlorella powder

Chlorella is a type of single-celled, water-grown micro-algae, widely known as a powerful superfood. It contains all of the B vitamins, Vitamin C, Vitamin E, beta-carotene, amino acids, magnesium, iron and other minerals. It binds to toxins and carries them out of the body. Chlorella cleanses the blood, optimizes oxygen and increases white blood cell count.

Cacao powder and nibs

Cacao contains many chemicals that enhance physical and mental wellbeing, including a rich supply of magnesium. Other minerals present in cacao are calcium, zinc, iron, copper and potassium. Cacao also contains more antioxidant flavonoids than red wine, green tea and blueberries. Cacao nibs are unprocessed, hulled cacao beans. See also page 40.

Carob powder

This has a chocolate-like flavour but contains no cacao and no caffeine. It comes from the dried pods of the carob tree and is a nutritious alternative to cocoa powder.

Cayenne pepper

Cayenne pepper fires up your metabolism and indirectly helps you burn more calories. It also helps to break up mucus and toxins, and stops cravings. It makes a perfect addition to dressings and drinks, including the cleansing Detox Lemonade on page 27.

Coconut oil or coconut butter

Coconut oil is a great multi-tasker. You can smear it, cook with it and eat it! It has powerful antibacterial and anti-viral properties and it makes a very effective moisturizer, and scalp and hair conditioner. I use it in smoothies, desserts and as a lip balm! In its solid state, it is coconut butter, so warm it gently to melt it. See also page 128.

Goji berries or wolfberries

These tasty, dried super-berries, similar in taste to savoury cranberries, are high in antioxidants, Vitamin C, beta-carotene and iron.

Himalayan pink salt

Himalayan pink salt is minimally processed, retains much of its natural mineral content and is highly alkalizing.

Maca powder

Maca powder comes from the Peruvian maca root. It contains Vitamin B1, B2, B12, C, and E, calcium, zinc, magnesium, iron, amino acids and complex carbohydrates. It is really good for balancing hormones and building muscle.

Maple syrup

A great natural sweetener with a unique caramel flavour, it consists primarily of sucrose and water. It also contains potassium, calcium, zinc, manganese and trace amino acids. See also page 136.

Nama shoyu

This is an unpasteurized soy sauce. Although it is heated well above the standard raw temperature limit, it still contains living enzymes.

Nutritional yeast

This is a deactivated yeast sold in flakes or powder. It is a source of protein and vitamins, especially B-complex, and is a complete protein. Sometimes it is fortified with Vitamin B12. It has a strong cheesy, nutty flavour and it is often used by vegans in place of cheese.

Oils

When buying olive, flaxseed (linseed), hemp, sesame or nut oils, look for the cold-pressed varieties. They come from the first press and are never heated or exposed to chemical processing, and because of that, they offer more nutritional value and a more intense flavour. Look for oils in dark glass bottles in the refrigerator section of your healthfood store. The recipes in this book sometimes call for extra virgin olive oil, and sometimes just olive oil – this is because some dishes benefit from a milder (ie. not extra virgin) taste.

Omega-3 oils

Omega-3 oils (or fatty acids) are polyunsaturated fatty acids which are considered essential because they cannot be synthesized by the human body but are vital for normal metabolism. They have been shown to lower the risk of cardiovascular disease. Common sources of Omega-3 oils include fish oils, hemp seed and flaxseed (linseed).

Seaweed

Seaweed offers a super-rich and easily absorbed source of minerals and vitamins, including iron, calcium, Vitamin B and A, potassium, iodine, zinc, selenium and copper. It helps to remove heavy metals and radioactive substances from our bodies. It is usually sold dried so it should be reconstituted by soaking in cold water before chopping up and sprinkling over salads. Types of edible seaweed include wakame, dulse, arame and nori sheets for sushi.

Spirulina powder

Spirulina is an algae and the highest natural protein food on the planet, with all of the essential amino acids required for optimum health. It contains, among other myriad benefits, 50 times more iron than is found in the same amount of spinach.

Tahini paste

A thick paste made from ground sesame seeds, tahini contains B vitamins, which promote healthy cell grow and division. It is also an excellent source of calcium. The recipes in this book call for raw (cool-milled within raw temperature boundaries) or light (ie. made from hulled, unroasted sesame seeds) tahini.

Water

I recommend that you use filtered water for sprouting, soaking, smoothies and any other recipe in this book that calls for water.

Nuts & seeds

Almonds
Almonds are the healthiest nuts, with calcium and magnesium for strong bones, Vitamin E and phytochemicals, which may help protect against cardiovascular disease and cancer. Almond milk is a great alternative to cow's milk. See also page 120.

Cashews
These mildly sweet nuts are packed with energy, antioxidants, minerals and vitamins. They are a good source of selenium, copper, zinc, Vitamin B5, Vitamin B6 and Vitamin B1. See also page 32.

Chia seeds
Chia seeds are not widely known in Europe but that is changing as people learn about this great energy food. They are rich in Omega-3 oils, including alpha-linolenic acid, fibre and essential minerals.

Flaxseeds or linseeds
Containing Omega-3, Omega-6 and Omega-9 fatty acids and soluble fibre, these seeds are high in lignans, known to balance hormone levels. Try adding a tablespoon of ground flaxseeds to your morning smoothie. The body cannot break down flaxseeds in their whole form, so be sure to grind them into a meal before using. See also page 92.

Pecans
Pecans are a good source of protein and Omega-6 fatty acids. The antioxidants and plant sterols found in pecans reduce high cholesterol.

Pine nuts
These are the edible seeds of pine trees. They are a good source of Vitamin K, E and B, fibre, and minerals including iron, magnesium and phosphorus.

Pumpkin seeds
Pumpkin seeds contain measurable amount of zinc, iron and calcium. They are an excellent snack food supplying protein and B-complex vitamins.

Sunflower seeds
These are very high in Vitamin E and are also a good source of Vitamin B1 and compounds called phytosterols, which are believed to reduce cholesterol, enhance the immunity and decrease the risk of certain cancers.

Walnuts
Walnuts have the highest content of Omega-3 oils among all tree nuts. See also page 61.

techniques & equipment

Soaking
All raw nuts are brought to life when placed in water, which dissolves their enzyme inhibitors and makes them more digestible. The harder the nut, the longer you need to soak it.

Sprouting
It's very easy to sprout beans, nuts, grains and seeds at home (see also page 12). You need a wide-mouth glass jar. Rinse the beans, nuts, grains or seeds, place in a bowl and cover with cold water. Set aside at room temperature overnight. The next day, rinse and drain them well. Place them in a glass jar, cover with a piece of muslin/ cheesecloth held in place with an elastic band, and tilt the jar slightly over a plate. Rinse with fresh water 3–4 times a day and keep away from direct sunlight. Beans such as lentils, azuki or mung beans can be sprouted in a colander. Eat sprouts when the growing tail is the length of the soaked seed and store them in the refrigerator. You can also buy a sprouter (with stacked trays) for this purpose. Once you have soaked your seeds, spread them evenly over the sprouter trays. The stacking system allows a healthy circulation of air around each layer of sprouts.

High-speed blender
Blenders are used for smoothies, sauces, dressings and grinding seeds. I highly recommend a Vitamix for fast and efficient preparation – it blends all sorts of ingredients, like frozen bananas, to perfect purées.

Food processor

A good-quality food processor like a Magimix is perfect for blitzing ingredients to a specific texture or consistency.

Dehydrator

A dehydrator replicates many of the qualities associated with cooked food, especially warmth and that familiar texture, without destroying the benefits of living, raw foods. I recommend the Excalibur brand with 9 shelves and a timer. The dehydrating times given in the recipes might vary depending on the humidity in your kitchen and the thickness and temperature of your ingredients, so please check your food frequently.

Juicers

There are 2 types of juicers on the market: masticating and centrifugal. A masticating juicer is necessary to juice green leafy vegetables, herbs and sprouts. It extracts the juice slowly, so the oxidation is much slower and more nutrients are released. The juice's shelf life is longer. A centrifugal juicer works by using a flat-cutting blade on the bottom of a rapidly spinning basket. This cannot break down leafy green vegetables and the juice is not as rich as that produced by a masticating juicer, but it is still good.

Spiralizer

This is a gadget designed to make vegetable 'noodles' or 'spaghetti'. A mandolin is also useful for fine, even shavings.

*de*tox programmes

Detox aids

Water
Remember to drinks lots of water during a detox – at least 2 litres/quarts per day if possible. You can also drink herbal teas, including fennel, nettle, and peppermint. Avoid caffeinated herbal teas and coffee where possible.

Exercise
Avoid strenuous exercise. Light exercise such as stretching, yoga or swimming is a valuable way of improving your circulation and thereby helping with elimination of toxins.

Natural products
Use natural personal care products such as face and body creams, shampoo and toothpaste, as well as natural household products where possible. This will help to create the best conditions for your body to cleanse because it will not have to cope with or be stressed by chemicals.

Dry skin brushing
This is a very effective addition to your cleansing programme because it helps to stimulate the lymphatic system. Use a natural vegetable bristle brush (available from a chemist or online) and always use it on dry skin, ideally before a bath or shower. A complete skin brushing should take about 4–5 minutes. Try to cover the whole body (except the face) when brushing. The direction of brushing should generally be towards the heart area.

Epsom salts
Relaxing in a warm bath of Epsom bath salts helps to draw out toxins from the blood and takes the stress off the liver and kidneys. Follow the manufacturer's instructions and soak yourself for 20 minutes. Afterwards, make sure that you wrap up warm and relax.

Complementary therapies
Sessions of massage and colonic hydrotherapy can help you get the most out of the cleansing process, especially if you think you are likely to, or find that you do, experience detox symptoms.

Detox symptoms

You may well sail through your detox feeling great. However, depending on your regular lifestyle, you might experience some detox symptoms. Typically, these are short lived. Below are some common symptoms and simple measures to help deal with them. If your symptoms appear to be severe or unusual please contact your doctor or other health professional as soon as possible.

Bad breath
The tongue is a fantastic diagnostic tool: a tongue coating indicates elimination of toxins (it will lessen over the week). Buy a tongue scraper from a chemist or use an old toothbrush to gently scrape the coating off your tongue each morning.

Fatigue
Your body is using its energy to support the detox process. You may also be eating less than you are used to. This is most likely to happen in the first few days of your cleanse so please do not worry! Try not to do anything which makes to many demands on your body – keep exercise light and rest as much as possible. Drink plenty of water.

Headaches or short-lived nausea
Toxins which have been stored in cells are being released into the bloodstream. You may also be experiencing withdrawal from caffeine or other stimulants. Keep drinking lots of water and stick to the programme in order to help your body get rid of the toxins. Try taking a bath with Epsom salts. Book a session of manual lymphatic drainage massage.

Skin rash
The body is eliminating toxins, and the skin is an important organ of elimination. This is unpleasant but try not to get upset as it will pass. Try colonic hydrotherapy or a lymphatic drainage massage. Keep drinking lots of water, stick to organic skincare products that will not irritate the skin and use a skin brush only very gently.

5-day cleansing detox

This programme is perfect for your first detox or if you are new to the raw-food regime. It is enjoyable and gentle while still offering you a beneficial level of cleansing. The process can help you to lose weight, boost your energy levels or get back on track with healthy eating after a time of excessive indulgence.

The food and juice programme graduates from a full, raw-food menu, through lighter eating of salads only, to the most intense part of a cleanse – a juice fast. After that, you reintroduce salads and then move to the full, raw-food menu. The complete structure of the programme is as follows.

Day 1

Full, raw-food menu including a dehydrated dish, salads, a smoothie, a lemonade and juices

Day 2

Salads, smoothies and juices

Day 3

Juice fast

Day 4

Salads, smoothies and juices

Day 5

Full, raw-food menu including a dehydrated dish, salads, a smoothie, a lemonade and juices

Day 1

7 am Start the day with warm water and lemon or ginger, or herbal tea

8 am Detox Lemonade (see page 27)

9.30 am Green Super-smoothie (see page 32)

11.30 am Green Veggie Juice (see page 27)

1.30 pm Parsnip 'Tabbouleh' (see page 53)

3.30 pm Carrot & Lemon Juice with Omega-3 Oils (see page 28)

6.30 pm Mushroom, Olive & Tomato Tartlets with Walnut Pastry (see page 99) and Apple, Cabbage & Raisin Salad (see page 58)

8 pm Herbal tea

--- --- --- --- --- --- --- --- --- --- --- ---

Day 2

7 am Start the day with warm water and lemon or ginger, or herbal tea

8 am Mint Lemonade (see page 44)

9.30 am Mango Smoothie with Turmeric (see page 39)

11.30 am Green Veggie Juice (see page 27)

1.30 pm Sprouted Buckwheat Salad (see page 54)

3.30 pm Apple, Fennel & Broccoli Juice (see page 28)

6.30 pm Carrot & Beet Salad with Walnuts (see page 69)

8 pm Green Veggie Juice (see page 27)

Day 3

7 am Start the day with warm water and lemon or ginger, or herbal tea

8 am Detox Lemonade (see page 27)

9.30 am Green Veggie Juice (see page 27)

11.30 am Carrot & Lemon Juice with Omega-3 Oils (see page 28)

1.30 pm Apple, Fennel & Broccoli Juice (see page 28)

3.30 pm Green Veggie Juice (see page 27)

6.30 pm Pineapple & Apple Juice with Spinach (see page 43)

8 pm Cucumber, Apple & Pear Juice with Watercress (see page 43)

--- --- --- --- --- --- --- --- --- --- --- --- ---

Day 4

7 am Start the day with warm water and lemon or ginger, or herbal tea

8 am Mint Lemonade (see page 44)

9.30 am Green Super-smoothie (see page 32)

11.30 am Green Veggie Juice (see page 27)

1.30 pm Thai Cabbage Salad (see page 69)

3.30 pm Carrot & Lemon Juice with Omega-3 Oils (see page 28)

6.30 pm Mock Tuna Salad with Olives (see page 65)

8 pm Cucumber, Apple & Pear Juice with Watercress (see page 43)

Day 5

7 am Start the day with warm water and lemon or ginger, or herbal tea

8 am Detox Lemonade (see page 27)

9.30 am Melon & Banana Smoothie with Parsley (see page 35)

11.30 am Green Veggie Juice (see page 27)

1.30 pm Parsnip 'Rice' Salad with Capers & Tomatoes (see page 73)

3.30 pm Carrot & Lemon Juice with Omega-3 Oils (see page 28)

6.30 pm Tomato Quiche with Almond Pastry (see page 83) and Kale Salad with Cranberries (see page 58)

8 pm Herbal tea

--- --- --- --- --- --- --- --- --- --- ---

5-day glow detox

This is a juice-based, 5-day cleansing detox that also includes a large salad, a nut milk and a smoothie every day. It has been specifically designed to reduce solid food intake and speed up the detox process without resorting to a juice-only regimen.

This particular plan delivers amazing results to the skin's appearance and improves your metabolism through the combination of organic green and fruit juices, bespoke smoothies and salads. Vitamins, minerals, enzymes, antioxidants and phytonutrients from the juices are easily assimilated straight to the bloodstream, simultaneously hydrating your body. Green leaves and green vegetables present in the juices and salads are high in Vitamins A, B, C, E and K, minerals such as iron, calcium, magnesium and potassium and natural sulphur to stimulate collagen production and keep skin smooth.

You will complete this detox feeling clear, energized, radiant and lean on the outside!

The complete structure of the programme is as follows.

First thing in the morning (around 7.30–8 am)
2 x servings of Detox Lemonade (see page 27)

Breakfast (around 9–9.30 am)
2 x servings of Green Veggie Juice (see page 27)

Mid-morning (around 11 am)
2 x servings of any smoothie

Lunch (around 1–2 pm)
any salad

Afternoon (around 3–4 pm)
2 x servings of any juice

Supper (around 6–7 pm)
2 x servings of Green Nut Milk (see page 31)

Evening (around 8–9 pm)
2 x servings of Detox Lemonade (see page 27)

3-day juice detox

This is a strict, liquid-only detox programme. You consume freshly made vegetable and fruit juices plus lemonades and nut milks with no solid foods at all. The juices provide the nutrients needed for liver detoxification. Green juices especially work hard to alkalize the body, quickly giving you optimum health. This is quite an intense programme designed for those who want to achieve quick results.

Not only will you lose weight, but your energy levels will also increase and your skin will glow!

You start and finish your day with a lemonade, have a nut milk for supper, and 3 juices during the day.

First thing in the morning (around 7.30–8 am)
2 x servings of Detox Lemonade (see page 27)

Mid-morning (around 11 am)
2 x servings of Green Veggie Juice (see page 27)

Lunch (around 1–2 pm)
2 x servings of Pineapple & Apple Juice with Spinach (see page 43)

Afternoon (around 3–4 pm)
2 x servings of Cucumber, Apple & Pear Juice with Watercress (see page 43)

Supper (around 6–7 pm)
2 x servings of Cashew Milk (see page 32)

Evening (around 8–9 pm)
2 x servings of Detox Lemonade (see page 27)

After a detox

It is important that you do not shock your body after the last day of a detox. You should introduce cooked food slowly, beginning with plant foods and choosing organic whenever possible.

The following is a guide to re-establishing your preferred eating pattern. It starts from the first day following the detox. The options listed are alternatives and you do not have to eat all of them! Please avoid alcohol and caffeine during the post-detox and if desired re-introduce these items in very small measures afterwards.

Day 1

Breakfast fruit salad, ideally including berries, served with natural/plain (unsweetened) yogurt (try sheep or goat yogurt); a fresh fruit smoothie made with berries and non-dairy milk (eg. almond, oat or rice)

Lunch large salad with green leaves, mixed raw vegetables, avocado and olives; steamed vegetables with cottage cheese or goat or sheep cheese, eg. feta. Use simple dressings such as extra virgin olive oil and lemon juice, or avocado or walnut oil.

Evening meal large salad with green leaves and/or steamed vegetables with hummus; brown rice, millet or quinoa with vegetables and olive oil dressing. No cheese if you have already had some at lunchtime. Stick to simple ingredients on Day 1.

Day 2

Breakfast non-wheat carbohydrate cereal eg. oat or millet porridge or wheat-free muesli with almond or rice milk; rice cakes or rye bread with mashed avocado or almond nut butter; fresh fruit salad with natural/plain (unsweetened) yogurt and a few nuts and seeds.

Lunch large salad with green leaves plus vegetable proteins such as beans, lentils or seeds; non-wheat grains eg. rice cakes, rice bread or oatcakes spread with nut butter, guacamole, vegetable pâté or hummus; boiled eggs and spinach on rye bread.

Evening meal plenty of vegetables, cooked or raw with a grain such as brown rice or quinoa and a small portion of fish, preferably steamed or grilled.

Day 3 onwards

By now you can eat more or less your 'normal' diet again. If you are a meat eater then a small portion of meat can be introduced on Day 3 but choose preferably chicken or turkey (or fish) rather than red meat at this stage.

juices & smoothies

Green Veggie Juice is the most beneficial of all the juices in this chapter – low in sugar, high in antioxidants and alkalizing. Detox Lemonade is rich in Vitamin C, and with the cayenne pepper, it warms the body and supports your digestive system.

green veggie juice

serves 2–3

1 cucumber

5 celery stalks/ribs

100 g/3½ oz. broccoli

¼ fennel bulb

½ courgette/zucchini

1 apple

1 lime, peeled

3 large handfuls of fresh parsley

3 large handfuls of spinach or kale

juicer

If you are using a masticating juicer, run all the ingredients through the juicer. If you using a centrifugal juicer, alternate leaves with the celery and apple to prevent them getting caught in the machine.

Divide the juice between 2–3 glasses and serve.

detox lemonade

serves 2

freshly squeezed juice of 2–3 large lemons

500 ml/2 cups water

20 ml/1½ tablespoons pure maple syrup

2 pinches of ground cayenne pepper

blender

Put all the ingredients in a blender and blitz.

Divide the lemonade between 2 glasses. Serve lightly chilled.

Like a glass of sunshine on a dull wintry morning, this sweet, vibrant juice will give you the boost you need to face the day.

carrot & lemon juice
with omega-3 oils

serves 2

1.2 kg/2¾ lbs. carrots

freshly squeezed juice of
2 lemons

2–4 teaspoons Omega-3
oils (eg. flaxseed oil or a
combination of flaxseed,
primrose and pumpkin oils),
to taste

juicer

Put the carrots in a juicer and blitz until all the juice is extracted. Whisk in the lemon juice and oils to taste until well mixed.

Divide the juice between 2 glasses and serve immediately.

Don't let the broccoli in this juice put you off trying it! Apple and the subtle aniseed taste of the fennel are what dominate.

apple, fennel & broccoli juice

serves 2

650 g/1½ lbs. apples (about
4 large apples)

200 g/7 oz. broccoli

250 g/9 oz. fennel (about
1 large fennel bulb)

1 lemon, peeled and pith
removed

juicer

Put all the ingredients in a juicer and blitz until all the juice is extracted.

Divide the juice between 2 glasses and serve immediately.

This bright green nut milk is surprisingly sweet and tasty. Try it – it's a great way to eat your greens!

green nut milk

serves 2–3

400 ml/1⅔ cups water

150 g/1 cup cashews

2 soft, pitted dates

1 teaspoon coconut oil

¼ teaspoon salt

1 large handful of spinach

blender

Put all the ingredients in a blender and blitz until completely smooth.

Divide the milk between 2–3 glasses and serve lightly chilled.

Fragrant, fruity and a fabulous pink-red colour, this is a lovely shake to enjoy in the summertime and beyond.

pineapple & strawberry shake
with maca powder

serves 3–4

500 ml/2 cups water

150 g/1 cup strawberries

160 g/1½ cups diced pineapple

2 ripe bananas, peeled and chopped

2 teaspoons maca powder

1 teaspoon pure vanilla extract

1 teaspoon coconut oil

a pinch of salt

blender

Put all the ingredients in a blender and blitz until completely smooth.

Divide the shake between 3–4 glasses. Serve immediately.

Cashew milk is very easy and quick to make, and it's a highly nutritious dairy-free drink. You will be surprised by how delicious it can taste!

cashew milk

serves 2

75 g/½ cup cashews

400 ml/1⅔ cups water

1–2 tablespoons agave nectar, to taste

½ teaspoon coconut oil

a pinch of salt

blender

Put all the ingredients in a blender and blitz until completely smooth.

Divide the milk between 2 glasses and serve immediately.

This green super-smoothie is the best way to increase your consumption of dark leafy greens, without even tasting them!

green super-smoothie

serves 2–3

2–3 ripe bananas, peeled and chopped

1 kiwi, peeled and chopped

2 handfuls of spinach

½ teaspoon chlorella powder (optional)

½ teaspoon spirulina powder (optional)

400 ml/1⅔ cups water

blender

Put all the ingredients in a blender and blitz until completely smooth.

Divide the smoothie between 2–3 glasses and serve immediately.

cashews are the kidney-shaped seeds that adhere to the bottom of the cashew apple, the fruit of the cashew tree. Cashews are delicately flavoured and are a good source of magnesium, phosphorus, copper and manganese.

This smoothie provides a powerful boost of vitamins, minerals, antioxidants and other nutrients. The melon seeds are high in Vitamin A and C. I especially recommend the cantaloupe melon, but any melon would be good.

melon & banana smoothie *with parsley*

serves 2–3

2 ripe bananas, peeled and chopped

200 g/7 oz. melon, peeled and cubed (seeds in)

1 handful of fresh parsley

freshly squeezed juice of 1 lime

1 teaspoon barley grass powder

500 ml/2 cups water

blender

Put all the ingredients in a blender and blitz until completely smooth.

Divide the smoothie between 2–3 glasses and serve immediately.

Fragrant, sweet and thick, this shake will fill you up and provide the ideal mix of anti-ageing antioxidants.

strawberry cashew shake *with goji berries*

serves 2–3

200 g/1½ cups strawberries

500 ml/2 cups water

50 g/⅓ cup cashews

2 large, ripe bananas, peeled and chopped

1 tablespoon goji berries

blender

Put all the ingredients in a blender and blitz until completely smooth.

Divide the shake between 2–3 glasses and serve immediately.

strawberries are an excellent source of folate, potassium, fibre, Vitamin C and manganese.

This smoothie might be a good alternative to your daily cup of coffee due to its stimulating properties. It will give you energy!

banana, berry & cacao smoothie

serves 2–3

3 ripe bananas, peeled and chopped

seeds and juice from 1 passionfruit

175 g/1 generous cup frozen berries, thawed

2 tablespoons raw cacao powder

1 tablespoon ground flaxseeds

1 tablespoon agave nectar or coconut sugar

400 ml/1⅔ cups water

blender

Put all the ingredients in a blender and blitz until completely smooth.

Divide the smoothie between 2–3 glasses and serve lightly chilled.

This lovely pick-me-up juice gently increases circulation and is full of natural sugars, Vitamin C and potassium.

apple, ginger & cinnamon juice

serves 2–3

8–9 large apples

2-cm/¾-inch piece of fresh ginger

1 teaspoon ground cinnamon

juicer

Put the apples and ginger in a juicer and blitz until all the juice is extracted. Stir in the cinnamon.

Divide the juice between 2–3 glasses. Serve immediately.

cinnamon has a long history as a spice and a medicine. It is a powerful antioxidant, helps control blood sugar levels and stops the growth of bacteria.

A zesty and rich blend of cashews, cacao and orange, this smoothie is sinfully delicious!

chocolate orange smoothie

serves 3

3 ripe bananas, peeled and chopped

4 soft, pitted dates

freshly squeezed juice of 1 orange

40 g/¼ cup cashews

1 tablespoon raw cacao powder

400 ml/1⅔ cups water

blender

Put all the ingredients in a blender and blitz until completely smooth.

Divide the smoothie between 3 glasses. Serve immediately.

Turmeric is a potent natural anti-inflammatory and it combines with carrot and mango to make this smoothie a punchy orange colour to brighten up your day!

mango smoothie *with turmeric*

serves 2

400 g/2 ripe mangos, peeled, pitted and cubed

5-cm/2-inch piece of fresh ginger, peeled and chopped

400 ml/1⅔ cups fresh carrot juice

1 teaspoon ground turmeric

freshly squeezed juice of ½ lime

blender

Put all the ingredients in a blender and blitz until completely smooth.

Divide the smoothie between 2 glasses. Serve immediately.

Enjoy this fibre-rich treat on cold winter mornings
to warm you up and sustain you until lunchtime.

winter spice smoothie
with maca powder

serves 3

2 ripe bananas, peeled and
chopped

1 pear, cored and chopped

½ apple, cored and chopped

1 teaspoon maca powder

1-cm/½-inch piece of fresh
ginger, peeled and chopped

½ teaspoon ground cinnamon

¼ teaspoon freshly ground
nutmeg

¼ teaspoon ground cloves

500 ml/2 cups water

blender

Put all the ingredients in a blender
and blitz until completely smooth.

Divide the smoothie between 3 glasses
and serve immediately.

cacao nibs are hulled
and crushed cacao beans. They
provide more antioxidant flavonoids
than green tea and blueberries.
They are an incredibly rich source
of magnesium and other essential
minerals like calcium, zinc, iron,
copper and potassium.

This is a chocolate lover's dream! Truly decadent, it
will keep your energy soaring throughout the day.

coco shake

serves 3

50 g/⅓ cup blanched almonds

3 ripe bananas, peeled and
chopped

1 tablespoon raw cacao
powder

1 tablespoon cacao nibs

1 generous teaspoon raw or
light tahini paste

3 soft, pitted dates

½ teaspoon ground cinnamon

400 ml/1⅔ cups water

blender

Put the almonds in a bowl, cover with
warm water and allow to soak for at least
3 hours to soften.

Thoroughly drain the almonds, put with
the remaining ingredients in a blender
and blitz until completely smooth.

Divide the shake between 3 glasses
and serve immediately.

Pineapple is a rich source of bromelain, an enzyme that helps to break down proteins and has anti-inflammatory properties.

pineapple & apple juice
with spinach

serves 2
5 apples
2 handfuls of spinach
1 handful of fresh mint
½ large pineapple, peeled
freshly squeezed juice of
1 lime
juicer

Put 1 apple in the chute of the juicer, followed by the spinach, mint and a piece of pineapple. Turn the juicer on and push through. Follow with the remaining ingredients, then whisk in the lime juice.

Divide the juice between 2 glasses and serve lightly chilled.

Here is a refreshing and tangy green juice that combines cooling cucumber with the tart taste of apples and watercress.

cucumber, apple & pear juice
with watercress

serves 2
3 apples
2 handfuls of watercress
1 large cucumber
2 pears
freshly squeezed juice of
1 lemon
juicer

Place 1 apple in the chute of the juicer, followed by the watercress. Turn the juicer on and push through. Follow with another apple and then the remaining ingredients. Whisk in the lemon juice.

Divide the juice between 2 glasses and serve lightly chilled.

I love the tangy, fruity flavour of this smoothie, with aromatic parsley in the background.

orange & banana smoothie
with watercress

serves 2–3
200 ml/¾ cup water
200 ml/¾ cup freshly squeezed orange juice
120 g/1 cup peeled, pitted and cubed mango
1 small, ripe banana, peeled and chopped
1 small handful of fresh parsley
1 handful of watercress

blender

Put all the ingredients in a blender and blitz until completely smooth.

Divide the smoothie between 2–3 glasses and serve immediately.

This uplifting lemonade stimulates the circulation, refreshes the body and enlivens the senses.

mint lemonade

serves 2
freshly squeezed juice of 1 lime
freshly squeezed juice of 1 lemon
400 ml/1⅔ cups water
1–2 tablespoons agave nectar, to taste
1 handful of fresh mint

blender

Put all the ingredients in a blender and blitz until completely smooth.

Strain the lemonade through a sieve/strainer and divide between 2 glasses. Serve lightly chilled.

watercress is a nutrient-rich perennial herb. It has a high concentration of Vitamin C: 100 g/3½ oz. of watercress provides 47 mg or 72% of your recommended daily allowance of Vitamin C. It is also an excellent source of Vitamin A and K and calcium, and it is rich in the B-complex group of vitamins.

salads & dressings

In this pretty, autumnal salad, chicory is paired with apple and walnuts and drizzled with a creamy dressing. With plenty of crunch and flavour, it is a twist on the French brasserie classic.

chicory & apple salad
with caramelized walnuts

serves 4

salt and freshly ground
black pepper

for the caramelized walnuts

50 g/⅓ cup walnut pieces,
soaked for 6 hours and
drained thoroughly

2 tablespoons pure maple
syrup or runny honey

for the salad

1 large apple

freshly squeezed juice of
½ lemon

200 g/7 oz. celeriac/celery
root, peeled and coarsely
grated

3 plump heads of chicory/
Belgian endive

Mustard Dressing (page 77)

non-stick dehydrator sheet
dehydrator

For the caramelized walnuts, first put the walnuts in a bowl of cold water and allow to soak for 6 hours.

After 6 hours, thoroughly drain the walnuts and put them in a bowl with the maple syrup or honey and ¼ teaspoon salt. Toss to coat the nuts, then spread them out on the dehydrator sheet. Dehydrate at 46°C/115°F for 12 hours or until crispy, turning them over halfway through dehydrating.

For the salad, core the apple, if you like, then slice it very thinly. Transfer to a bowl with the lemon juice and celeriac/celery root, and toss to coat in the lemon juice. Set aside.

Separate the chicory/endive leaves and put them in a mixing bowl. Pour the Mustard Dressing over the leaves. Add the apple and celeriac. Toss with a spoon and fork so that all the ingredients get coated. Taste for seasoning. Divide between plates and sprinkle with the caramelized walnuts. Serve straightaway.

chicory or Belgian endive is a perennial plant native to Europe, India and Egypt. The leaves are used as a vegetable, and the roasted root as a caffeine-free coffee substitute. Chicory root contains vitamins and minerals, the polysaccharide inulin and volatile oils. It is used in natural medicine to regulate the heartbeat and help with diabetes. It also helps to tone and detoxify the liver.

This is full of the fresh, light taste of summer – with the distinctive fragrances of basil and mint – but still leaves you feeling satisfied thanks to the pine nuts and capers.

fennel salad
with herbs & capers

serves 2

1 fennel bulb

2 large handfuls of rocket/arugula

2 tablespoons capers, rinsed and drained

1 tablespoon pine nuts

freshly squeezed juice of ½ large lemon

2 tablespoons extra virgin olive oil

salt and freshly ground black pepper

6 fresh basil leaves, chopped

6 fresh mint leaves, chopped

1 handful of fresh parsley, chopped

Trim the fennel and shave it or slice it very thinly.

Place the fennel in a bowl with the rocket/arugula, capers and pine nuts. Add the lemon juice, olive oil and salt and pepper, to taste. Mix well, then toss in the herbs.

fennel is a vegetable often praised as a digestive aid. It is high in antioxidants, Vitamin C, fibre, folate and potassium, which helps to lower high blood pressure, in turn reducing the chances of strokes and heart attacks. It has also been shown to have anti-inflammatory qualities.

Tabbouleh is a popular Middle Eastern salad made with bulghur wheat. In this clever wheat-free version, parsnip successfully replaces the bulghur but you don't lose any of the fresh flavours from the herbs and lemon juice.

parsnip *'tabbouleh'*

serves 4

2 large parsnips, peeled and cubed

1 cucumber

3 large tomatoes, seeded

60 g/2 large handfuls of fresh parsley

15 g/1 small handful of fresh mint

freshly squeezed juice of 1½ lemons

3 tablespoons olive oil

salt and freshly ground black pepper

Put the parsnips in a food processor and pulse a few times until finely chopped to resemble grains of bulghur wheat. Transfer to a bowl.

Dice the cucumber and tomatoes and finely chop the herbs. Add to the bowl and stir together.

Add the lemon juice, olive oil and salt and pepper, to taste. Mix well.

Leave the salad in the fridge for at least 1 hour, or overnight if possible, to allow the flavours to develop.

mint is a herb with a cool, rich pungent flavour and aroma. Mint may help with indigestion and headaches. It is an excellent source of Vitamin C, which helps to boost the immune system.

This fibre-rich salad is deliciously light, but that does not mean it will leave you feeling hungry! You will need to start sprouting the buckwheat 3–4 days in advance.

sprouted buckwheat salad

serves 2–4

100 g/⅔ cup raw buckwheat

50 g/2 handfuls of spinach leaves, roughly chopped

3 large tomatoes, seeded and diced

1 cucumber, seeded and diced

1 red (bell) pepper, seeded and diced

1 handful of fresh dill, chopped

1 handful of fresh chives, snipped

1 handful of rocket/arugula

Dill Vinaigrette (page 79)

large glass jar

Soak the buckwheat in plenty of cold water overnight – it will roughly double in size.

The next day, place the soaked buckwheat in a fine-mesh sieve/strainer and rinse with cold water to get rid of any starchiness. Drain. Place the buckwheat in the large glass jar to sprout. Rinse and drain at least 3 times a day. The sprouts should be ready in 3 days, depending on the weather – it might take less time in warmer climates.

When you are ready to make the salad, combine the buckwheat sprouts with the spinach, tomatoes, cucumber, (bell) pepper, dill and chives. Serve on a bed of the rocket/arugula with the Dill Vinaigrette.

buckwheat – not in fact a type of wheat – is a seed from a plant related to rhubarb and sorrel. It is a very good source of iron, manganese, magnesium, copper and dietary fibre. It is a complete protein, containing all eight essential amino acids.

Here is a healthy spin on a classic Caesar salad, with a wonderful dressing that tastes creamy thanks to the cashews.

celeriac 'caesar' salad
with olives & pine nuts

serves 2

salt and freshly ground black pepper

for the 'caesar' dressing

100 ml/6 tablespoons extra virgin olive oil

50 ml/3 tablespoons water

1–2 garlic cloves, peeled

1 celery stalk/rib, chopped

2 tablespoons cashews

2 tablespoons pure maple syrup

2 tablespoons nama shoyu (unpasteurized soy sauce)

for the salad

600 g/1¼ lbs. celeriac/celery root, peeled and coarsely grated

1 large head of romaine lettuce, shredded

3 tablespoons freshly squeezed lemon juice

4 tablespoons pine nuts

120 g/¾ cup pitted green olives, halved

For the 'Caesar' dressing, put all the ingredients in a food processor or blender and blend until smooth. Season to taste.

For the salad, put the celeriac/celery root, lettuce, lemon juice and a pinch of salt in a bowl and stir well. Add the pine nuts and olives and toss well together.

Serve immediately with the 'Caesar' dressing.

celeriac or celery root is the root of a particular variety of celery. It is very low in calories, high in Vitamin K and a good source of some essential minerals such as phosphorus, potassium and manganese.

This is one of the simplest and healthiest salads you can make, and it's a tasty way to enjoy kale.

kale salad *with cranberries*

serves 2

200 g/7 oz. kale, stalks removed

freshly squeezed juice of ½ lime

1 tablespoon extra virgin olive oil

salt

60 g/½ cup dried cranberries

Avocado Dressing (page 74)

Very finely chop the kale. Put in a bowl with the lime juice and olive oil. Add salt, to taste, and massage the kale for a few minutes.

Add the cranberries, then allow the kale to marinate for 30 minutes.

Serve with the Avocado Dressing.

This is a fresh-tasting and flavourful slaw made from crunchy cabbage, tangy apples and sweet raisins.

apple, cabbage & raisin salad

serves 4

200 g/7 oz. Savoy cabbage, cored

200 g/7 oz. red cabbage, cored

1–2 apples, cored

2 tablespoons raisins

Almond Sauce (page 75)

salt and freshly ground black pepper

Very finely shred the cabbages and grate the apples. Put them in a large bowl with the raisins and mix well.

Add the Almond Sauce (you may only need about half of it), season to taste and allow to marinate for 30 minutes before serving.

All the rainbow colours come together here to create a wonderful taste! Additionally, the walnuts and wild rice provide bags of nutrition and an interesting texture.

rainbow salad *with wild rice*

serves 4

130 g/¾ cup wild rice

1 large carrot, julienned

1 red (bell) pepper, seeded and julienned

1 small raw beet(root), peeled and julienned

½ small sweet potato, peeled and julienned

1 handful of fresh dill, chopped

1 handful of fresh parsley, chopped

½ teaspoon grated lemon zest

½ teaspoon grated orange zest

salt and freshly ground black pepper

1 handful of rocket/arugula

Citrus Dressing (page 76)

Caramelized Walnuts (page 49)

Put the wild rice in a bowl of cold water and allow to soak overnight.

The next day, thoroughly drain the rice and put in a bowl with the carrot, (bell) pepper, beet(root), sweet potato, dill, parsley and lemon and orange zests. Mix well and season to taste.

Serve on a bed of the rocket/arugula with the Citrus Dressing and Caramelized Walnuts.

walnuts are rich in Omega-3 fatty acids, Vitamin E and many other antioxidants and anti-inflammatory nutrients.

This is a super-healthy dish that offers a refreshing combination of sweet potatoes, (bell) pepper and courgette/zucchini mingled with a hint of chilli.

sweet potato & courgette salad
with arame & bean sprouts

serves 4

15 g/½ oz. dried arame

2 sweet potatoes, peeled

2 courgettes/zucchini

1 red (bell) pepper, seeded

1 handful of fresh coriander/cilantro

100 g/¾ cup fresh corn kernels (about 1 cob/ear)

50 g/1½ oz. azuki bean sprouts (or mung bean sprouts or any other bean sprouts)

1 tablespoon olive oil

salt

Chilli & Lime Dressing (page 78)

spiralizer (optional)

Soak the arame in a bowl of cold water for 10–15 minutes.

Meanwhile, spiralize the potatoes and courgettes/zucchini using the spiralizer, then cut the ribbons into shorter pieces. If you do not have a spiralizer, cut the potatoes into julienne strips and shave the courgettes/zucchini into ribbons using a vegetable peeler. Thinly slice the (bell) pepper and roughly chop the coriander/cilantro.

Thoroughly drain the arame. In a bowl, toss all the prepared ingredients together with the olive oil and salt, to taste. Allow to marinate for 30 minutes.

Serve with the Chilli & Lime Dressing.

sprouts are one of the most alkalizing and nutritious foods on the planet. They are abundant in all essential amino acids, vitamins, minerals, chlorophyll and enzymes. Sprouts are very easy to digest for optimum assimilation of nutrients.

This is a clever vegan answer to tuna cravings and full
of appealing textures and colours.

mock tuna salad *with olives*

serves 4

watercress or rocket/arugula,
to serve

salt and freshly ground black pepper

for the mock tuna

120 g/1 cup walnuts

120 g/1 cup sunflower seeds

1 celery stalk/rib, finely chopped

1 carrot, peeled and grated

1 handful of fresh dill, chopped

for the tomato mayo sauce

75 g/⅔ cup cashews

3 tablespoons water

1 tomato, chopped

¼ red onion, chopped

1 garlic clove, peeled and chopped

2 tablespoons freshly squeezed
lemon juice

1 tablespoon nutritional yeast
(optional)

1 teaspoon agave nectar

½–1 teaspoon mustard powder

for the topping

1 courgette/zucchini, finely diced

1 cucumber, finely diced

2 large tomatoes, diced

100 g/¾ cup pitted kalamata or
black olives, sliced

1 handful of fresh parsley, chopped

3 tablespoons extra virgin olive oil

Soak the walnuts and sunflower seeds for the mock tuna in
a bowl of cold water, and the cashews for the tomato mayo
sauce in a separate bowl of cold water for 30 minutes.

For the mock tuna, thoroughly drain the walnuts and seeds
and place them in a food processor. Blitz them to a smooth
paste, adding a little water if necessary. Transfer to a bowl
and add the celery, carrot and dill. Mix well, season to taste
and set aside.

For the tomato mayo sauce, thoroughly drain the cashews
and put in a blender or food processor with the remaining
ingredients. Blend until completely smooth and runny, adding
a little more water if necessary. Transfer to the mock tuna
and stir well. Season to taste.

For the topping, combine all the ingredients and season
to taste.

To serve, place the mock tuna on a bed of watercress or
rocket/arugula and scatter the topping over everything.

The healthy fats in avocado will do wonders for your skin and help to give you a clear and glowing complexion!

avocado & tomato salad
with red pepper chilli dressing

serves 4

150 g/1 generous cup cherry or baby vine tomatoes, halved

1 small handful of spinach

1 red onion, thinly sliced

1 handful of fresh coriander/ cilantro, chopped

1 handful of fresh parsley, chopped

2 ripe avocados, peeled, pitted and thickly sliced

1 handful of pumpkin seeds

for the red pepper chilli dressing

75 g/½ cup cashews

1 red (bell) pepper, seeded and chopped

1 fresh red or green chilli

1 teaspoon ground paprika

⅓ red onion, chopped

freshly squeezed juice of 1 lemon

1 tablespoon nama shoyu (unpasteurized soy sauce)

salt and freshly ground black pepper

For the red pepper chilli dressing, soak the cashews in a bowl of cold water for 30 minutes.

Thoroughly drain the cashews and put in a food processor or blender with the remaining ingredients. Blend until smooth and creamy.

Put the tomatoes, spinach, onion, coriander/ cilantro, parsley and avocados in a bowl and toss with the red pepper chilli dressing.

Divide the salad between 4 plates and top with the pumpkin seeds.

avocado is the fruit of a tall evergreen tree native to Central and South America. It provides nearly 20 essential nutrients including fibre, potassium, Vitamin E, B-vitamins and folic acid.

Bursting with flavour and texture, this Thai version of cabbage slaw is very easy to prepare. It is the perfect dish for the Asian-food lover.

thai cabbage salad

serves 2–3

½ small Savoy cabbage, cored

1 carrot

Thai Dressing (page 77)

4–6 leaves of romaine lettuce

1 small handful of fresh coriander/cilantro, chopped

Very finely chop the cabbage, and peel and coarsely grate the carrot. Mix together, then stir through enough Thai Dressing to coat. Divide the mixture between the lettuce leaves and scatter over the coriander/cilantro.

Alternatively, serve the Thai Dressing in a little bowl on the side so that people can help themselves.

This is a super-easy salad with a piquant mustard dressing that would suit an autumnal or wintry lunch.

carrot & beet salad
with walnuts

serves 2

2 carrots

1 beet(root)

1 handful of walnuts, quartered

Mustard Dressing (page 77)

2 big handfuls of rocket/arugula

Peel and coarsely grate the carrots and beet(root). Mix with the walnuts and stir through enough Mustard Dressing to coat.

Serve the mixture on a bed of the rocket/arugula.

This is a complete, healthy meal in a bowl – a blend of seeds, nuts, vegetables and sprouts tossed in a mustard dressing.

nut *'rice'* & crunch salad

serves 4

100 g/⅔ cup walnuts

100 g/⅔ cup sunflower seeds

2 celery stalks/ribs, thinly sliced

1 red (bell) pepper, seeded and julienned

1 large carrot, julienned

½ cucumber, julienned

1 big handful of salad leaves

Mustard Dressing (page 77)

1 handful of alfalfa and sunflower seed sprouts, or any other variety of sprouts

Soak the walnuts in a bowl of cold water for 2 hours, and the sunflower seeds in a separate bowl of cold water for 30 minutes.

Thoroughly drain the walnuts and sunflower seeds when they have been soaked. Put them in a food processor and blitz until finely chopped. Transfer to a bowl with the celery, (bell) pepper, carrot and cucumber.

Serve on a bed of the salad leaves with the Mustard Dressing and the sprouts scattered over the top.

For a delightful change from real rice, try this medley
of earthy parsnip, juicy tomatoes and sharp, salty capers.

parsnip *'rice'* salad
with capers & tomatoes

serves 3–4

2 parsnips, peeled and roughly chopped

150 g/1 generous cup cherry tomatoes, halved

2 tablespoons capers, rinsed and drained

1 courgette/zucchini, diced

2 big handfuls of rocket/arugula

Balsamic Vinaigrette (page 76)

salt and freshly ground black pepper

Put the parsnips in a food processor and pulse briefly a few times until they are finely chopped like rice. Transfer to a bowl and add the tomatoes, capers and courgette/zucchini. Stir well.

Add the rocket/arugula and gently toss, then stir through enough Balsamic Vinaigrette to coat. Season to taste.

balsamic vinegar is an Italian vinegar made from white Trebbiano grapes, which are particularly sweet. It is fermented and aged in wooden barrels over a number of years to produce a distinctively mellow, dark vinegar that gives a rich sweetness to salad dressings.

salad dressings & sauces

This collection of healthy dairy- and wheat-free salad dressings make any salad taste amazing. They are simple to prepare and taste great!

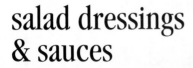

avocado dressing

serves 2

1 ripe avocado, peeled, pitted and roughly chopped

freshly squeezed juice of 1 lemon

3 tablespoons olive oil

salt and freshly ground black pepper

3–6 tablespoons water

Put all the ingredients in a food processor or blender and blend, gradually adding the water until you get a creamy consistency.

nut 'mayo'

makes about 300 ml/1¼ cups
150 g/1 cup cashews
200 ml/¾ cup water
1½ tablespoons nutritional yeast
(optional)
½–1 teaspoon apple cider vinegar
salt

Put all the ingredients in a food
processor or blender and blend
until smooth and creamy.

almond sauce

makes about 400 ml/1⅔ cups
3 celery stalks/ribs, roughly chopped
125 g/½ cup raw almond butter
(if not available, use non-raw)
3 tablespoons freshly squeezed lemon juice
(from about 1 large lemon)
1 handful of fresh parsley, chopped
1 garlic clove, peeled
½ teaspoon salt
freshly ground black pepper

Put all the ingredients in a food processor
or blender and blend until quite smooth,
adding a little water if necessary.

balsamic vinaigrette

makes about 250 ml/1 cup

120 ml/½ cup extra virgin olive oil

60 ml/¼ cup organic balsamic vinegar

1½ tablespoons nama shoyu
(unpasteurized soy sauce)

1½ tablespoons apple cider vinegar

1½ tablespoons pure maple syrup

Put all the ingredients in a screw-top
jar and shake well until emulsified.
Shake or stir again before serving.

tahini sauce

makes about 300 ml/1¼ cups

3 tablespoons raw or light tahini

1 garlic clove, peeled

freshly squeezed juice of 3 lemons

2 tablespoons apple cider vinegar

1 tablespoon extra virgin olive oil

1½ tablespoons pure maple syrup

100 ml/½ cup water

¼ teaspoon Himalayan pink salt,
or to taste

Put all the ingredients in a food
processor or blender and blend
until smooth and creamy. Stir again
before serving.

citrus dressing

makes about 350 ml/1½ cups

freshly squeezed juice of 1 orange

freshly squeezed juice of 1 lemon

1 tablespoon nama shoyu
(unpasteurized soy sauce)

1 tablespoon agave nectar

¼ fresh red chilli, seeded and chopped

1-cm/⅝-inch piece of fresh ginger,
peeled and chopped

150 ml/⅔ cup extra virgin olive oil

Put all the ingredients in a food
processor or blender and blend until
smooth. Stir again before serving.

mustard dressing

makes about 250 ml/1 cup

200 ml/¾ cup safflower oil

60 ml/¼ cup white wine vinegar

1½ tablespoons Dijon mustard

Himalayan pink salt and freshly ground
black pepper

Put all the ingredients in a screw-top jar
and shake well until emulsified. Shake or
stir again before serving.

thai dressing

makes about 450 ml/2 cups

100 g/⅔ cup cashews

freshly squeezed juice of 3 lemons

1.5-cm/⅜-inch piece of fresh ginger,
peeled and chopped

½ fresh red chilli, chopped (seeds in)

3 tablespoons extra virgin olive oil

1 tablespoon nama shoyu
(unpasteurized soy sauce)

50 ml/3 tablespoons pure maple syrup

100 ml/½ cup water

Put all the ingredients in a food
processor or blender and blend until
smooth. Stir again before serving.

ginger shoyu marinade

makes about 550 ml/2¼ cups

300 ml/1¼ cups sesame oil (cold-pressed, unrefined and untoasted)

50 ml/3 tablespoons nama shoyu (unpasteurized soy sauce)

50 ml/3 tablespoons agave nectar

freshly squeezed juice of 5 limes

1 garlic clove, peeled

1 red chilli, chopped (seeds in)

2-cm/¾-inch piece of fresh ginger, peeled and chopped

1 small handful of fresh coriander/cilantro, chopped

salt

Put all the ingredients in a food processor or blender and blend until smooth.

chilli & lime dressing

makes about 450 ml/2 cups

100 ml/½ cup freshly squeezed lime juice (from about 3 large limes)

300 ml/1¼ cups sesame oil (cold-pressed, unrefined and untoasted)

1½ tablespoons agave nectar

1½ tablespoons nama shoyu (unpasteurized soy sauce)

½ red chilli, finely chopped (seeds in or out, as you like)

Put all the ingredients in a screw-top jar and shake well until emulsified. Shake or stir again before serving.

chilli peppers contain numerous health-giving compounds, such as capsaicin, Vitamin C, Vitamin A and flavonoid antioxidants. Capsaicin, which gives chillies their strong, spicy, pungent character, has antibacterial, anti-carcinogenic and antidiabetic properties. Chillies are a good source of minerals like potassium, manganese, iron and magnesium, and also of B-complex vitamins such as niacin, Vitamin B6 and Vitamin B1.

dill vinaigrette

makes about 250 ml/1 cup

150 ml/⅔ cup olive oil

75 ml/⅓ cup freshly squeezed lemon juice

1 teaspoon Dijon mustard

½ tablespoon runny honey

2 teaspoons white wine vinegar

1 handful of fresh dill, finely chopped

3 tablespoons water

salt and freshly ground black pepper

Put all the ingredients in a screw-top jar and shake well until emulsified. Shake or stir again before serving.

mains

This savoury tart features both fresh and sun-dried tomatoes within a crisp, nutty crust – wheat and dairy free!

tomato quiche *with almond pastry*

serves 8

salt and freshly ground black pepper

rocket/arugula, to serve (optional)

for the pastry dough

300 g/2 cups blanched almonds

2 tablespoons olive oil

for the filling

80 g/⅔ cup sun-dried tomatoes

4 large tomatoes

1 fresh red chilli

2 tablespoons balsamic vinegar

2 tablespoons pure maple syrup

225 g/1½ cups cashews

25-cm/10-inch loose-based tart pan

non-stick dehydrator sheet

dehydrator

For the pastry dough, soak the almonds in a bowl of cold water for 6 hours.

Thoroughly drain the almonds and put in a food processor with the olive oil. Blitz until almost smooth, then add water, a teaspoon at a time, and keep blitzing until a sticky dough forms. Season to taste.

Transfer the pastry dough to the tart pan. Push the dough evenly over the base and side of the pan with your fingers to make a neat shell. Put the tart on the dehydrator sheet and dehydrate at 46°C/115°F for about 4–5 hours or until the pastry is dry.

For the filling, soak the sun-dried tomatoes in a bowl of cold water for 15 minutes.

Thoroughly drain the sun-dried tomatoes, then put in a food processor with the fresh tomatoes, chilli, vinegar and maple syrup. Blitz to a mousse consistency. Add the cashews and blitz again until smooth. Season to taste.

Spoon the filling into the dehydrated tart shell and level with the back of a spoon. Serve immediately with rocket/arugula, if liked.

In this recipe, sweet potato and courgette/zucchini are spiralized to make noodle-shaped strips and to create an original and satisfying meal.

vegetable *'noodles'*

serves 2

1 red (bell) pepper, seeded

½ bok choy

½ courgette/zucchini

1 sweet potato, peeled

salt

3 spring onions/scallions, sliced

1 generous handful of fresh coriander/cilantro, chopped

freshly squeezed juice of ½ lime

Tahini Sauce (page 76) or Thai Dressing (page 77)

sesame seeds, to sprinkle

spiralizer (optional)

Very thinly slice or julienne the (bell) pepper. Thinly slice the bok choy. Spiralize the courgette/zucchini and sweet potato using the spiralizer, if you have one. If you don't have one, shave the courgette/zucchini into ribbons using a vegetable peeler and julienne the sweet potato.

Combine all the prepared vegetables in a bowl, sprinkle a generous pinch of salt over them and gently toss together. Allow to rest at room temperature for 15–30 minutes.

When you are ready to serve the 'noodles', add the spring onions/scallions, coriander/cilantro and lime juice. Serve with Tahini Sauce or Thai Dressing and a scattering of sesame seeds.

sweet potatoes are high in Vitamin C, Vitamin B6 and iron. They also contain Vitamin D, which is critical for a healthy immune system. Sweet potatoes are also a good source of magnesium, which helps to promote relaxation and combat stress.

Try this interesting take on one of the world's most popular noodle dishes. Raw courgette/zucchini 'noodles' are tossed with crunchy vegetables and green Thai paste.

green *'pad thai'*

serves 2–3

salt

for the garnish

2½ tablespoons cashews

1 tablespoon agave nectar or pure maple syrup

1 teaspoon olive oil

¼ teaspoon chilli powder

for the green thai paste

2½ tablespoons cashews

1 lemongrass stalk, chopped

50 g/⅔ cup raw coconut chips

1 tablespoon freshly squeezed lime juice

1 tablespoon chopped fresh ginger

½–1 fresh green chilli, chopped

2 spring onions/scallions, white part and 2 cm/¾ inch of green part, chopped

1 big handful of fresh basil, torn into pieces

1 teaspoon mild curry powder

4 tablespoons coconut water or water

for the marinade

1½ tablespoons sesame oil (cold-pressed, unrefined and untoasted)

1 spring onion/scallion, chopped

1 tablespoon agave nectar

¼ fresh red chilli, chopped

2-cm/¾-inch piece of fresh ginger, peeled and chopped

1 tablespoon freshly squeezed lemon juice

1 garlic clove, peeled

for the 'pad thai'

1 large courgette/zucchini

1 bok choy, thinly sliced

1 red (bell) pepper, seeded and thinly sliced

1 small carrot, julienned

50 g/⅔ cup sliced shiitake mushrooms

non-stick dehydrator sheet

dehydrator

spiralizer (optional)

For the garnish, toss all the ingredients together with a pinch of salt, then spread them out on the dehydrator sheet. Dehydrate at 46°C/115°F for 20 hours.

For the green Thai paste, soak the cashews in a bowl of cold water for 30 minutes. Thoroughly drain the cashews, then put in a blender with all the remaining green Thai paste ingredients and ½ teaspoon salt. Blitz until smooth, adding more water if needed.

For the marinade, put all the ingredients in the blender and blitz until smooth.

For the 'pad Thai', spiralize the courgette/zucchini using the spiralizer, if you have one. If you don't have one, shave the courgette/zucchini into ribbons using a vegetable peeler. Put the courgette/zucchini in a bowl, then stir in enough green Thai paste to coat the ribbons. Allow to marinate for 30 minutes. Meanwhile, put the bok choy, (bell) pepper, carrot and mushrooms in a bowl. Pour the marinade over and mix well. Allow to marinate for 30 minutes.

To serve, divide all the vegetables between 2–3 plates and garnish with the cashews.

The deep colours of this dish are amazing. It is a powerful medley of red cabbage (high in protective phytonutrients), antioxidant-rich pomegranate and cleansing fennel and beet(root).

red cabbage & fennel
with pomegranate & pecans

serves 2

¼ small red cabbage, cored

½ fennel bulb

1 small beet(root), peeled

1 handful of pecans

freshly squeezed juice of
½ lemon

½ pomegranate

salt and freshly ground
black pepper

Nut 'Mayo' (page 75)

1 handful of spinach

Very thinly slice the cabbage, shave the fennel (reserving the fronds) and coarsely grate the beet(root). Put them in a bowl with the pecans and fennel fronds, pour the lemon juice over and mix well. Allow to marinate for about 15 minutes.

Scoop the pomegranate seeds out of the skin and add the seeds to the bowl. Season to taste.

Serve on a bed of the spinach with the Nut 'Mayo'.

pomegranate is one of the oldest cultivated fruits. It contains no fat, is low in sugar and rich in fibre, Vitamin C, K and B5, potassium, zinc and folic acid, which helps to repair DNA and create healthy blood cells. High in antioxidants, it may counteract cellular damage due to free radicals.

This is a feast of textures and colours! Make sure you leave everything to marinate for a full hour to allow the flavours to develop and the vegetables to soften slightly.

raw stir-fry

serves 4

6 cobs/ears of baby sweetcorn
½ red (bell) pepper, seeded
¼ Savoy cabbage, cored
1 small carrot, peeled
½ courgette/zucchini
75 g/⅔ cup sugar snap peas
1–2 broccoli stalks
75 g/1 cup sliced shiitake mushrooms
Ginger Shoyu Marinade (page 78)
salt and freshly ground black pepper
1 big handful of pea shoots

Thinly slice the sweetcorn, (bell) pepper and cabbage. Julienne the carrot and the courgette/zucchini. Slice the sugar snap peas diagonally. Divide the broccoli into small florets and chop finely.

Put all the prepared vegetables in a bowl with enough Ginger Shoyu Marinade to coat well. Refrigerate and allow to marinate for 1 hour.

Season to taste and serve with the pea shoots.

Dehydrated flatbread made from seeds and onions creates a really interesting pizza crust. Cover it with non-dairy cashew cheese and a tomato-based topping for a gorgeous evening meal.

pizza cruda

serves 4

salt and freshly ground black pepper

Red Onion Bread (page 106), made in a disc

for the topping

50 g/⅓ cup sun-dried tomatoes

1 courgette/zucchini, finely diced

4 large tomatoes, diced

3 Portobello mushrooms, diced

1 red (bell) pepper, seeded and diced

½ red onion, finely chopped

2 tablespoons extra virgin olive oil

1 tablespoon balsamic vinegar

1 teaspoon dried oregano

for the cashew cheese

75 g/½ cup cashews

1 tablespoon nutritional yeast (optional)

2 tablespoons freshly squeezed lemon juice

3 tablespoons water

For the topping, soak the sun-dried tomatoes in a bowl of cold water for 10 minutes. Thoroughly drain the tomatoes and slice them, then put them in a large bowl with the remaining topping ingredients. Season to taste and set aside.

For the cashew cheese, soak the cashews in a bowl of cold water for 30 minutes. Thoroughly drain the cashews, then put them in a food processor with the remaining cashew cheese ingredients. Blitz until you get a smooth, thick, spreadable paste, adding a little more water if necessary. Season well.

To serve, cut the Red Onion Bread into wedges and spread cashew cheese over them. Finish with the topping and serve immediately.

golden flaxseeds are one of the most powerful plant foods on the planet. They may help reduce the risk of heart disease, cancer, stroke and diabetes, so try them in this inventive pizza crust.

Going raw doesn't have to mean missing out on pasta!
Use a spiralizer to make spaghetti out of courgettes/
zucchini, then top with a raw puttanesca-style sauce.

vegetable *'spaghetti'*
with puttanesca sauce

serves 2

2 small courgettes/zucchini

50 g/⅓ cup pitted black olives, chopped

puttanesca sauce

50 g/⅓ cup sun-dried tomatoes

150 g/1 cup cherry tomatoes or baby plum tomatoes

1 garlic clove, crushed

1 teaspoon dried oregano

1 teaspoon dried basil

a pinch of ground cayenne pepper

2 tablespoons extra virgin olive oil

salt and freshly ground black pepper

spiralizer (optional)

For the puttanesca sauce, soak the sun-dried tomatoes in a bowl of cold water for 10 minutes.

Spiralize the courgettes/zucchini using the spiralizer, if you have one. If you don't have one, shave the courgettes/zucchini into ribbons using a vegetable peeler.

Thoroughly drain the tomatoes, then put in a food processor fitted with an 'S' blade. Add all the remaining puttanesca ingredients and process until smooth. Season to taste.

Divide the 'spaghetti' between 2 plates, top with the puttanesca sauce and garnish with the olives.

garlic has been used for both medicinal and culinary purposes for years. It is good for the heart and immune system thanks to its antioxidant properties, and it also helps to maintain healthy blood circulation.

This is the perfect recipe for a summer evening when it is too hot for a traditional heavy pasta meal.

vegetable *'pappardelle'* *with walnut pesto*

serves 4

2 large courgettes/zucchini

1 handful of sun-dried tomatoes

for the walnut pesto

3 handfuls of rocket/arugula

50 g/⅓ cup walnuts

150 ml/⅔ cup extra virgin olive oil

2 tablespoons water

2 tablespoons nutritional yeast (optional)

1–2 garlic cloves, peeled

freshly squeezed juice of ½ lemon

salt and freshly ground black pepper

Shave the courgettes/zucchini into ribbons using a vegetable peeler.

Soak the sun-dried tomatoes in a bowl of cold water for 10 minutes.

For the walnut pesto, put all the ingredients in a food processor or blender. Blitz until well combined but still slightly chunky. Season to taste.

Thoroughly drain the sun-dried tomatoes and slice them if they are large.

Divide the 'pappardelle' between 4 plates, top with the walnut pesto and garnish with the sun-dried tomatoes.

sun-dried tomatoes are ripe tomatoes that are placed in the sun to remove most of the water content. After this, the tomatoes keep their nutritional value. Tomatoes are high in lycopene, antioxidants and Vitamin C.

Meaty Portobello mushrooms are tossed in olive oil and dehydrated for an amazing sauté-style topping on these lovely tartlets encased in a walnut crust.

mushroom, olive & tomato tartlets
with walnut pastry

makes 3

salt and freshly ground black pepper

for the pastry dough

150 g/1 cup walnuts

2½ tablespoons sun-dried tomatoes

for the filling

3 large Portobello mushrooms, sliced

6 tablespoons extra virgin olive oil

150 g/1 cup pitted black olives

3 large tomatoes, roughly chopped

1 red onion, chopped

1 tablespoon balsamic vinegar

3 x 10-cm/4-inch tartlet pans
non-stick dehydrator sheet
dehydrator

For the pastry dough, soak the walnuts in a bowl of cold water for 3 hours, and the sun-dried tomatoes in a separate bowl of warm water for 15 minutes.

Thoroughly drain the walnuts and tomatoes and place in a food processor. Blitz until smooth, adding water if necessary to make a soft but not wet dough. Season to taste. Divide the dough into 3 and transfer each portion to a tartlet pan. Push the dough evenly over the base and side of each pan with your fingers to make a neat shell.

For the filling, mix the mushrooms with 2 tablespoons of the olive oil. Season to taste, then spread them out on the dehydrator sheet. Dehydrate at 46°C/115°F for at least 2 hours until they are soft and taste like sautéed mushrooms. Set aside.

Blitz the olives and 2 tablespoons of the olive oil in the food processor until coarse. Set aside. Now blitz the fresh tomatoes, onion and the remaining olive oil in the food processor until chunky. Transfer to a bowl, season with salt, then allow to rest for 30 minutes. After 30 minutes, drain the excess liquid, add the vinegar and season to taste.

Gently pop the tartlet shells out of the pans. Fill the shells with a layer of olives, then a layer of tomato salsa, then the dehydrated mushrooms. Serve immediately.

This recipe was created by Be, who manages the Raw Fairies kitchen. It's a triple-green feast of peppery rocket/arugula, pungent parsley and cleansing celery.

triple-green tartlets *with almond pastry*

makes 4

salt and freshly ground
black pepper

for the pastry dough

180 g/1⅓ cups blanched
almonds

for the filling

5–6 celery stalks/ribs,
chopped

115 g/½ cup raw almond
butter (if not available, use
non-raw)

2 big handfuls of rocket/
arugula, plus extra to serve

1 big handful of fresh parsley

2 tablespoons freshly
squeezed lemon juice

2 garlic cloves, peeled

4 x 10-cm/4-inch tartlet pans

For the pastry dough, soak the almonds in a bowl of warm water for at least 3 hours.

Thoroughly drain the almonds and put them in a food processor with a splash of water. Blitz until smooth and sticky, adding more water if necessary. Season with a pinch of salt. Divide the dough into 4 and transfer each portion to a tartlet pan. Push the dough evenly over the base and side of each pan with your fingers to make a neat shell. Refrigerate for 30 minutes.

For the filling, put all the ingredients in a food processor or blender and blitz until smooth. Season to taste.

Gently pop the tartlet shells out of the pans. Spoon the filling into the tartlet shells and level with the back of a spoon. Refrigerate for at least 1 hour. Serve with rocket/arugula on top.

snacks

This is a deliciously simple pâté that looks wonderfully dramatic. You will find that it has a pleasing kick from the chilli and fresh ginger.

beet pâté

serves 4

1 beet(root)

1 small red (bell) pepper, seeded

½ fresh red chilli

1 tablespoon peeled and chopped fresh ginger

200 g/1⅓ cups cashews

2 tablespoons olive oil

2 tablespoons nama shoyu (unpasteurized soy sauce)

2 tablespoons apple cider vinegar

1 tablespoon pure maple syrup

salt

Peel the beet(root) and chop into 2-cm/¾-inch chunks, and roughly chop the (bell) pepper and chilli.

Put all the ingredients in a food processor and blitz until very smooth.

Serve chilled, with crackers.

beet(root) is an excellent source of folic acid, niacin (Vitamin B3), Vitamin B6, Vitamin B5, iron, manganese and magnesium. The unique pigment antioxidant present in the root may offer protection against coronary artery disease, lower cholesterol and have anti-ageing effects.

Perfect for snack time, these crackers are packed with pumpkin seeds, which contain minerals including zinc, magnesium and iron.

seeded crackers

makes 9

125 g/½ cup ground golden flaxseeds

100 g/⅔ cup sunflower seeds, ground

100 g/⅔ cup pumpkin seeds, ground

20 g/¾ oz. nori flakes (optional)

2 tablespoons olive oil

salt and freshly ground black pepper

non-stick dehydrator sheet

dehydrator

Combine all the ingredients in a bowl, adding as much water as needed to form a relatively smooth paste. Season the mixture to taste with salt and pepper.

Using a spatula, spread the paste out on the dehydrator sheet to a rectangle about 1 cm/½ inch thick. Slice into 9 squares and dehydrate at 46°C/115°F for at least 20 hours until dry and crispy.

When the tops of the crackers are dry, flip the dehydrator sheet over and carefully peel it away. Put the crackers back on the sheet, upside down, and dehydrate further until the other side is dry. Store them in an airtight container until needed.

This is an easy, flavourful seeded bread made with onions to add an extra taste and a little moisture. The bread can be used to make sandwiches, or eaten with dips or on its own.

red onion bread

makes 9 pieces

2 red onions, peeled

125 g/½ cup ground golden flaxseeds

100 g/⅔ cup sunflower seeds, ground

1½ tablespoons nama shoyu (unpasteurized soy sauce)

50 ml/3 tablespoons extra virgin olive oil

non-stick dehydrator sheet
dehydrator

Very thinly slice the onions by hand or using the fine slicing blade of a food processor.

Mix all the ingredients in a bowl. Add up to 6 tablespoons water and stir to combine, adding more water if necessary to achieve a paste. Do not add too much water, as it will make the dehydration take longer.

Using a spatula, spread the paste out on the dehydrator sheet to a rectangle about 1 cm/½ inch thick. Slice into 9 squares and dehydrate at 46°C/115°F for at least 20 hours, flipping the pieces over halfway through. The bread is ready when it is dry on both sides. Store it in an airtight container until needed.

Slightly sweet with a touch of chilli and cumin, these irresistible almonds are a perfect afternoon snack!

spicy almonds

150 g/1 cup almonds
1 tablespoon pure maple syrup
2–2½ teaspoons chilli powder or cayenne pepper
1½ teaspoons minced or finely grated onion
¾ teaspoon ground cumin
½ teaspoon salt
non-stick dehydrator sheet dehydrator

Soak the almonds in a bowl of cold water for 6 hours.

Thoroughly drain the almonds, then toss them with all the remaining ingredients in a bowl to coat evenly.

Spread the almonds out on the dehydrator sheet. Dehydrate at 46°C/115°F for 24 hours, flipping them over halfway through. The almonds are ready when they are crunchy. Store them in an airtight container until needed.

This trail mix is a very satisfying blend of nuts, seeds and succulent fruits – great for snacking and sharing around.

salty trail mix

100 g/⅔ cup sunflower seeds
100 g/⅔ cup pecans
100 g/⅔ cup almonds
50 g/⅓ cup pumpkin seeds
3 tablespoons goji berries
3 tablespoons raisins
2–3 tablespoons pure maple syrup
1 teaspoon salt, or to taste
mesh dehydrator screen dehydrator

Soak the almonds and pecans in separate bowls of cold water for 4 hours; and the sunflower seeds and pumpkin seeds in separate bowls of cold water for 30 minutes.

Thoroughly drain all the nuts and seeds and toss them with all the remaining ingredients in a bowl. Add more salt, to taste.

Spread the mix out on the mesh dehydrator screen. Dehydrate at 46°C/115°F for 20–24 hours, flipping the mix over halfway through. It is ready when the nuts and seeds are crunchy. Store in an airtight container until needed.

Inspired by Mediterranean and Turkish cuisine, this is a very
quick dip to make. Serve it with crackers or crudités at a party.

courgette hummus

serves 2

1 courgette/zucchini, chopped

1½ tablespoons raw or light tahini

2 tablespoons freshly squeezed
lemon juice

1 tablespoon olive oil

1 small garlic clove, peeled

salt and ground cumin, to taste

Put all the ingredients in a food processor or blender
and blend until smooth.

Serve chilled, with crackers or crudités.

These vibrant crackers are high in fibre, low in carbohydrates,
crunchy and nutritious.

italian flaxseed crackers

makes 9

4–5 sun-dried tomatoes

80 g/⅔ cup cherry tomatoes

½ red (bell) pepper, seeded and
chopped

1 garlic clove, peeled

a pinch of chilli powder

1 teaspoon dried oregano

160 g/⅔ cup ground golden
flaxseeds

salt and freshly ground
black pepper

non-stick dehydrator sheet
dehydrator

Soak the sun-dried tomatoes in a bowl of cold water
for 15 minutes.

Thoroughly drain the sun-dried tomatoes, then put them
in a food processor with the cherry tomatoes, (bell)
pepper, garlic, chilli powder and oregano. Blitz until
smooth. Add the ground flaxseeds and blitz again until
just combined, adding water if necessary to achieve a
spreadable consistency. Season to taste.

Using a spatula, spread the paste out on the dehydrator
sheet to a rectangle about 1 cm/½ inch thick. Slice
into 9 squares and dehydrate at 46°C/115°F for about
9 hours. When the tops of the crackers are dry, flip the
dehydrator sheet over and carefully peel it away. Put
the crackers back on the sheet, upside down, and
dehydrate for a further 3 hours until the other side is
dry. Store them in an airtight container until needed.

Here is another ultra-quick dip to encourage you to stop eating the ready-made stuff and start making your own. It makes a tasty party appetizer.

herb, spinach & avocado dip

serves 2

1 ripe avocado, pitted

1 tablespoon freshly squeezed lime juice

1 teaspoon salt, or to taste

3 handfuls of baby spinach, stalks removed

3 tablespoons fresh parsley, finely chopped

1 tablespoon freshly snipped chives

Scoop the flesh from the avocado into a food processor. Add the remaining ingredients and blitz until nearly smooth.

Serve chilled, with crackers.

These fantastic, wholesome crackers are packed with seeds, courgettes/zucchini, tomatoes and kale. You'll love them!

vegetable crackers

makes 16

150 g/1 cup cherry tomatoes

2 garlic cloves, peeled

½ bunch of fresh chives

1 small courgette/zucchini, chopped

2 handfuls of kale, chopped

2 handfuls of spinach, chopped

1 tablespoon freshly squeezed lemon juice

3 tablespoons olive oil

60 g/½ cup sun-dried tomatoes

½ red onion, peeled

70 g/½ cup pumpkin seeds, ground

70 g/½ cup sunflower seeds, ground

120 g/½ cup ground golden flaxseeds

non-stick dehydrator sheet

dehydrator

Put the cherry tomatoes, garlic, chives, courgette/zucchini, kale, spinach, lemon juice, olive oil, sun-dried tomatoes and onion in a food processor and blitz until very finely chopped.

Transfer to a bowl, then stir in all the ground seeds until very well mixed. If the mixture is too dry to come together, add a little water to achieve a spreadable paste.

Using a spatula, spread the paste out on the dehydrator sheet to a rectangle about 1 cm/½ inch thick. Slice into 16 squares and dehydrate at 46°C/115°F for about 15 hours, flipping the pieces over halfway through. The crackers are ready when they are dry on both sides. Store them in an airtight container until needed.

This pâté requires so few ingredients to create a surprisingly complex flavour.

mushroom pâté

serves 3–4

3 large Portobello mushrooms, sliced

2–3 tablespoons olive oil

salt and freshly ground black pepper

150 g/1 cup cashews

1 tablespoon yeast flakes (optional)

non-stick dehydrator sheet

dehydrator

For the filling, mix the mushrooms with 2 tablespoons of the olive oil. Season to taste, then spread them out on the dehydrator sheet. Dehydrate at 46°C/115°F for at least 2 hours until they are soft and taste like sautéed mushrooms. Set aside.

Soak the cashews in a bowl of cold water for 30 minutes.

Thoroughly drain the cashews and put in a food processor with the mushrooms and yeast flakes, if using. Blitz to a paste and season to taste.

Serve chilled, with crackers.

Flaxseed crackers are a popular snack for those on a raw-food diet and these are particularly good with their Mexican spices.

mexican flaxseed crackers

makes 9

½ red (bell) pepper, seeded and chopped

60 g/½ cup cherry tomatoes

½ small red onion, chopped

1 garlic clove, peeled

1 teaspoon ground cumin

1 teaspoon ground coriander

a pinch of ground cayenne pepper

160 g/⅔ cup ground golden flaxseeds

1 tablespoon raw cacao powder

1 tablespoon olive oil

salt

non-stick dehydrator sheet

dehydrator

Put the (bell) pepper, tomatoes, onion, garlic, cumin, coriander and cayenne in a food processor. Blitz until smooth. Add the ground flaxseeds, cacao powder and olive oil and blitz again until combined. Transfer to a bowl and add salt, to taste. Add a little water if necessary to achieve a sticky dough.

Using a spatula, spread the paste out on the dehydrator sheet to a rectangle about 1 cm/½ inch thick. Slice into 9 squares and dehydrate at 46°C/115°F for about 9 hours. When the tops of the crackers are dry, flip the dehydrator sheet over and carefully peel it away. Put the crackers back on the sheet, upside down, and dehydrate for a further 3 hours until the other side is dry. Store them in an airtight container until needed.

sweets & desserts

The combination of creamy cashew coconut filling and sweet fragrant strawberries makes this a delicious summertime dessert.

strawberry tartlets *with walnut pastry*

makes 3–4

4 strawberries, sliced

for the pastry dough

150 g/1 cup walnuts

2 soft, pitted dates

1 tablespoon pure maple syrup

for the cashew coconut cream

150 g/1 cup cashews

20 g/¼ cup coconut chips

3 tablespoons water

1 tablespoon coconut oil

3–4 soft, pitted dates

1 teaspoon pure vanilla extract

¼ teaspoon salt

3–4 x 9-cm/3½-inch tartlet pans

For the pastry dough, soak the walnuts in a bowl of cold water for 30 minutes, and for the cashew coconut cream, soak the cashews in a separate bowl of cold water for 30 minutes.

For the pastry dough, thoroughly drain the walnuts and put in a food processor with the remaining pastry dough ingredients. Pulse until combined and sticky, adding water if necessary. Divide the dough into 3 or 4 and transfer each portion to a tartlet pan. Push the dough evenly over the base and side of each pan with your fingers to make a neat shell. Refrigerate for 30 minutes.

For the cashew coconut cream, thoroughly drain the cashews and put in the food processor with the remaining cashew coconut cream ingredients. Blitz until smooth.

Gently pop the tartlet shells out of the pans. Spoon the filling into the shells and level with the back of a spoon. Decorate with the strawberry slices and refrigerate until ready to serve.

coconut is highly nutritious and particularly rich in fibre and potassium, as well as many minerals.

Rich, dark and decadent, this is a healthful chocolate tart. Although coffee is not strictly 'raw', I am not a believer in taking the raw regime to extremes, so some coffee in an otherwise raw dessert is fine with me!

mocha torte *with cacao almond pastry*

serves 6–8

for the pastry dough

300 g/2 cups almonds

4 soft, pitted dates

2 tablespoons raw cacao powder

1–2 tablespoons pure maple syrup

a pinch of salt

for the filling

300 g/2 cups cashews

140 g/¾ cup coconut oil

200 ml/¾ cup fresh espresso coffee

75 g/¾ cup raw cacao powder, plus extra to dust

125 ml/½ cup pure maple syrup

1 teaspoon pure vanilla extract

deep, 23-cm/9-inch tart pan

For the pastry dough, soak the almonds in a bowl of cold water for 6 hours or overnight.

Thoroughly drain the almonds and put in a food processor with the dates, cacao powder, maple syrup and salt. Blitz to a smooth and thick paste. It may be necessary to scrape the side of the food processor with a spatula and continue to blend. Transfer the pastry dough to the tart pan. Push the dough evenly over the base and side of the pan with your fingers to make a neat shell. Refrigerate for 30 minutes.

For the filling, put all the ingredients in the food processor. Blitz until smooth, then pour into the tart shell. Refrigerate for at least 2 hours before serving. Dust with extra cacao powder.

almonds are among the most nutritious nuts. They are rich in fibre, vitamins such as Vitamin E, minerals such as manganese, potassium, calcium, iron, magnesium, zinc and selenium, and monounsaturated fatty acids.

As well as being simple, pretty after-dinner treats, these truffles make great pick-me-up snacks that will energize and nourish you, and give you a sweet boost when you need it most – mid-morning.

carob coconut truffles

makes about 24

150 g/1 cup walnuts, plus extra, finely chopped, to coat

60 g/¾ cup coconut chips, plus extra to coat

140 g/1¼ cups soft, pitted dates

4 tablespoons/¼ cup raw carob powder (or raw cacao powder, or a mixture of both)

2 teaspoons coconut oil

petits fours cases (optional)

Put all the ingredients in a food processor and blitz to a smooth paste.

Divide the paste into 24 pieces and shape each piece into a ball using your hands. The heat from your hands will help to soften the paste and mould it into neat balls.

Roll some of the truffles in the finely chopped walnuts, and others in the coconut chips. Leave the remaining truffles plain. Refrigerate for 1 hour before serving.

Place the truffles in petits fours cases, if liked.

This rich and creamy recipe uses only a few ingredients and is packed with healthy fats. Avocado and cacao create a perfect match.

chocolate avocado mousse *with raspberry coulis*

serves 4–6

100 g/¾ cup soft, pitted dates

1 teaspoon pure vanilla extract

1 tablespoon coconut oil

3 ripe avocados, pitted

50 g/scant ½ cup raw carob powder (or any light version of carob)

50 g/scant ½ cup raw cacao powder

150 g/1 generous cup raspberries, plus extra to serve

1 tablespoon agave nectar, or to taste

Soak the dates in a bowl of cold water for 10 minutes.

Thoroughly drain the dates and put in a food processor with the vanilla extract and coconut oil. Blitz until smooth. Scoop the flesh from the avocados into the food processor and add the carob and cacao powders. Blitz again until well combined.

Divide the mousse between 4–6 small ramekins and refrigerate for at least 30 minutes while you make a raspberry coulis.

To make the raspberry coulis, put the raspberries in the food processor or a blender and blitz to a purée. Strain through a sieve/strainer to get rid of the pips and stir in enough agave syrup to taste.

Serve the mousses with raspberries and the raspberry coulis on the side.

Chia seeds soaked in cashew milk turn into a simple dessert. The combination of complete protein, vitamins, minerals and Omega-3 oil works together to make sure you get a steady flow of energy all day long.

chia pudding

serves 2

100 g/⅔ cup chia seeds

300 ml/1¼ cups Cashew Milk (page 32)

¼ teaspoon ground cinnamon

agave nectar or pure maple syrup, to taste

blueberries, to serve

Place the chia seeds in a bowl, pour the milk over it and add the cinnamon. Stir until well mixed – the milk should completely cover the seeds. Set aside for 15 minutes or until all the milk has been absorbed by the seeds. Add more milk if the mixture is too thick and stir again.

Add agave nectar or maple syrup to taste and serve with blueberries.

blueberries are a good source of Vitamin C, Vitamin K and fibre. The colour of blueberries is produced by a group of flavonoids called anthocyanins, which have remarkable antioxidant power. Blueberries are believed to help fight ageing, combat disease, lower blood pressure and protect the heart and brain.

Take five ingredients and blitz yourself a raw, vegan chocolate brownie – a healthy way to satisfy a chocolate craving!

brownie squares

makes 6 large portions

300 g/2 cups cashews

120 g/¾ cup walnuts

110 g/1 cup raw cacao powder

100 g/⅔ cup soft, pitted dates

1 tablespoon coconut oil

agave or pure maple syrup, to taste (optional)

deep, 22 x 15-cm/8¾ x 6-inch baking pan or container, lined with parchment paper (optional)

Put all the ingredients in a food processor and blitz until they are well combined and you have a smooth and rather sticky paste. If it is too dry, add 2 or more tablespoons of agave or maple syrup.

Scrape the mixture into the prepared baking pan and smooth level with your hands. If you don't have the correct size of pan, lay a sheet of clingfilm/plastic wrap on a board, scrape the mixture onto the sheet and shape it with your hands into a rough rectangle about 2.5 cm/1 inch thick. Wrap in clingfilm/plastic wrap.

Refrigerate for 1 hour before cutting into 6 squares to serve.

coconut oil or butter (in its solid form) is extracted from the kernel or meat of matured coconuts. The naturally occurring saturated fat in coconut oil is actually good for you and provides a number of health benefits including increasing the metabolism and boosting your thyroid.

This is just mildly sweet – all the sugar comes from the maple syrup and the fruits. It will soon become your healthiest and most satisfying morning bowl of cereal.

ultra-healthy granola

150 g/1 cup almonds

100 g/⅔ cup pecans

4 tablespoons/¼ cup sunflower seeds

½ apple, cored and chopped

1 ripe banana, peeled and chopped

7 soft, pitted dates

4 tablespoons/¼ cup pure maple syrup

2 teaspoons freshly squeezed lemon juice

1 teaspoon ground cinnamon

2 teaspoons coconut oil

a pinch of salt

2 tablespoons raisins

1 tablespoon goji berries

non-stick dehydrator sheet dehydrator

Soak the almonds in a bowl of cold water for 4 hours; the pecans in a separate bowl of cold water for 2 hours; and the sunflower seeds in a third bowl for 2 hours.

Put the apple, banana, dates, maple syrup, lemon juice, cinnamon, coconut oil and salt in a food processor. Thoroughly drain the sunflower seeds and add 1 tablespoon of them to the food processor. Blitz to a smooth paste and transfer to a mixing bowl.

Thoroughly drain the almonds and pecans. Put them, along with the remaining sunflower seeds and the raisins, in the food processor and pulse briefly to coarsely chop them. Transfer to the mixing bowl, add the goji berries and stir until very well mixed with the paste.

Spread the granola out on the dehydrator sheet. Dehydrate at 46°C/115°F for 8 hours, then flip the granola over and dehydrate for a further 6–8 hours or until crunchy.

Break the granola into small pieces and store in an airtight container until needed. Serve with berries and nut milk.

A health-conscious lifestyle really does extend to eating desserts! This not only fits the bill, but also makes a lovely summer dessert for a dinner with friends.

berry tartlets *with almond pastry*

makes 4

berries, to serve

for the pastry dough

150 g/1 cup almonds

1 tablespoon pure maple syrup, or to taste

a pinch of salt

for the filling

150 g/1 cup cashews

100 g/¾ cup frozen berries (mixed forest fruits are ideal), thawed

100 g/6 tablespoons coconut oil

2 tablespoons pure maple syrup

1 teaspoon pure vanilla extract

4 x 10-cm/4-inch tartlet pans

For the pastry dough, soak the almonds in a bowl of cold water for 6 hours or overnight, and for the filling, soak the cashews in a separate bowl of cold water for 1 hour.

For the pastry dough, thoroughly drain the almonds and put in a food processor with the maple syrup and salt. Blitz until you get tiny granules, adding water only if needed. Divide the dough into 4 and transfer each portion to a tartlet pan. Push the dough evenly over the base and side of each pan with your fingers to make a neat shell. Refrigerate for 15 minutes.

For the filling, thoroughly drain the cashews and put in the food processor with the remaining ingredients. Blitz until completely smooth.

Gently pop the tartlet shells out of the pans. Spoon the filling into the tartlet shells and refrigerate for at least 2 hours. Serve with berries on top.

This lemon cookie is delightfully tender with the refreshing flavour of lemon – it's truly delicious and completely wheat-, dairy- and sugar-free!

lemon cashew cookies

makes 8–10

300 g/2 cups cashews

6 soft, pitted dates

4 tablespoons freshly squeezed lemon juice

1 teaspoon grated lemon zest

2 tablespoons pure maple syrup

1 tablespoon coconut oil

a pinch of salt

non-stick dehydrator sheet dehydrator

Soak the cashews in a bowl of cold water for 30 minutes.

Thoroughly drain the cashews and put in a food processor with the remaining ingredients. Pulse until well combined and still chunky. Divide the dough into 8–10 pieces and shape each piece into a round about 1.5 cm/ $\frac{5}{8}$ inch thick.

Arrange the cookies on the dehydrator sheet and dehydrate at 46°C/115°F for at least 20 hours until dry but still soft inside.

Store in an airtight container in the fridge until needed.

These cute cookies combine the creaminess of pecans with the intense sweetness of dates. They're guaranteed to please everyone!

pecan cookies

makes 8

240 g/1½ cups pecans

6 soft, pitted dates

2 tablespoons pure maple syrup

1 tablespoon coconut oil

½ teaspoon ground cinnamon

¼ teaspoon salt

non-stick dehydrator sheet
  dehydrator

Soak the pecans in a bowl of cold water for 1 hour.

Thoroughly drain the pecans and put in a food processor with the remaining ingredients. Pulse until well combined and still chunky. Divide the dough into 8 pieces and shape each piece into a round about 1.5 cm/ ⅝ inch thick.

Arrange the cookies on the dehydrator sheet and dehydrate at 46°C/115°F for 15–20 hours until dry but still soft inside.

Store in an airtight container in the fridge until needed.

maple syrup is a great natural sweetener and an excellent source of manganese and zinc, which are important allies in the immune system.

stockists & suppliers

Healthfood stores and farmers' markets are the best places to find fresh, seasonal, local and organic fruits and vegetables. However, many of the ingredients can be purchased online or from wholesalers.

Whole Foods Market stores can be found across the USA, Canada and the UK. Visit your local store for a wealth of excellent natural and organic produce.

UK

www.infinityfoods.co.uk
Telephone: 01273 603563
Fantastic Brighton store selling a huge range of healthy products including nuts, seeds, good oils and seaweed.

www.fresh-network.com
The one-stop resource for all things related to raw food and holistic health, eg. seeds for sprouting, oils, cacao nibs, lucuma powder, raw tahini, chia seeds, nori sheets and lots more.

www.vitamix.co.uk
Manufacturer of excellent high-speed blenders.

www.juiceland.co.uk
Online supplier of all equipment associated with a healthy lifestyle, including juicers, dehydrators, spiralizers and sprouters.

www.ukjuicers.com
Another online supplier of all equipment associated with a healthy lifestyle, including juicers, dehydrators, spiralizers and sprouters.

US

www.therawfoodworld.com
Ojai, California's The Raw Food World Store (also a TV show and blog) covers it all. Great online store with ingredients, blenders, deydrators, cookware and even some prepared foods.

www.sunfood.com
Sunfood Superfoods is a vast supplier of certified organic raw foods and non-GMO superfoods. Order online or buy their products in stores.

www.livingtreecommunity.com
Selling, among others, the very best organic tahini and other raw nut butters, Living Tree Community Foods is a Berkeley CA institution.

www.tropicaltraditions.com
For virgin organic coconut oil produced in small batches from fresh coconuts.

www.highvibe.com
Online supplier of natural, organic whole foods and nutritional products, such as raw cashew butter, agave nectar, maca powder, nutritional yeast, goji berries, apple cider vinegar and nama shoyu.

index

acknowledgments

I would like to thank my husband, for his love and patience, and encouraging my passion.

My parents for their emotional support and my sister, Be, for all her help and amazing skills.

Tina Agnew for being a loyal friend and for her belief in Raw Fairies' vision.

I am deeply grateful to all the people who have worked at Raw Fairies, especially to Ye, Si, Luke, Rick, Neo, Roberto, Martins, Maiko and Sean for their dedication and enthusiasm.

Special thanks to Cindy Richards for the opportunity to write this book and Céline Hughes for energy spent on editing the book, Iona Hoyle for a beautiful design, and William Lingwood for the great photography.